Introducing

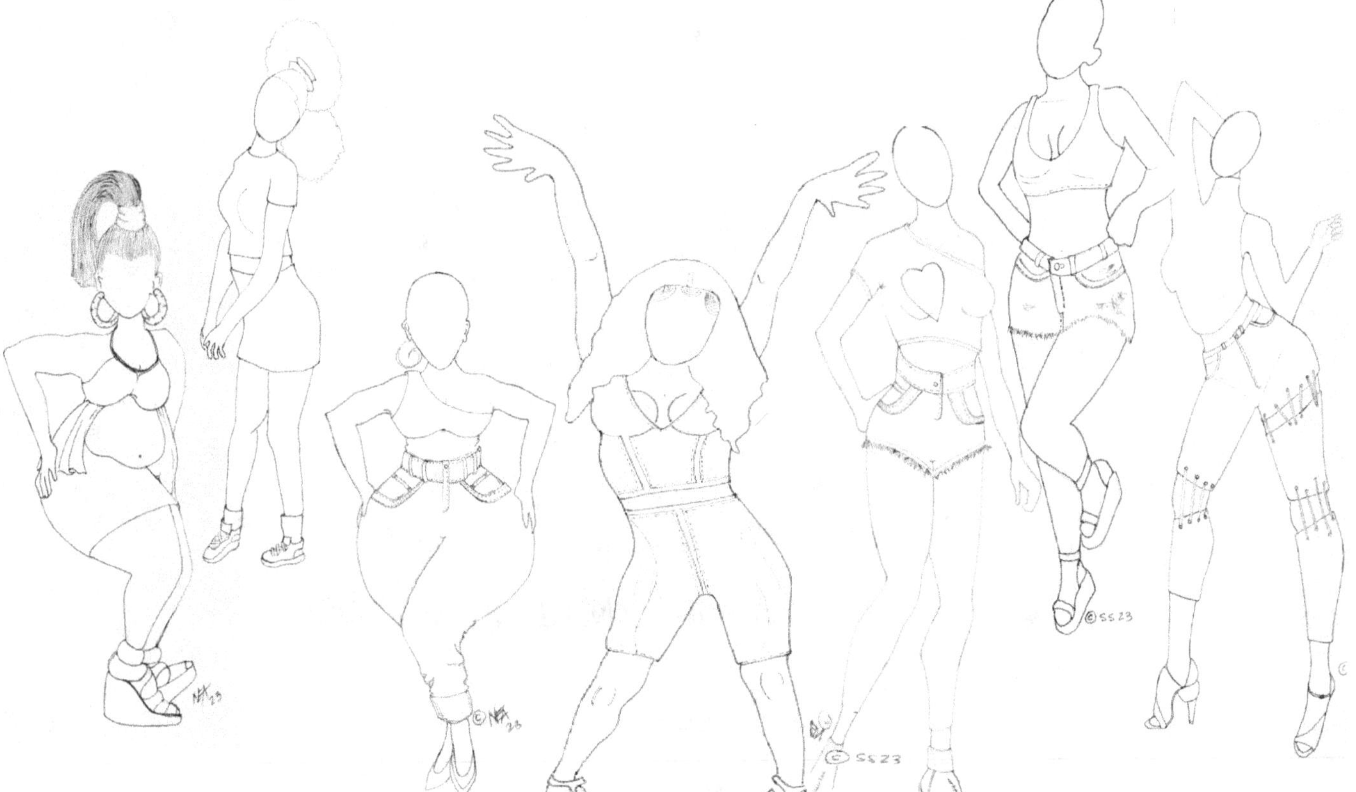

BLACK GIRL GLORY™

BLACK GIRL GLORY™

BROADWAY EMPIRE, LLC

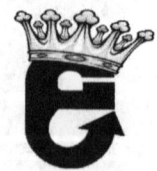

ISBN: 978-1-960826-10-7 (Paperback)

BE Publishing,
A division of Broadway Empire, LLC
Bronx NY 10472
broadwaympire@gmail.com
broadwayempire.com
Broadway Empire is a media and publishing company.
Printed in the United States of America

About the Artists

Dr. Nicole Elaine Avery was a drawing instructor at Phineas Banning High School (LAUSD) before obtaining an MFA in costume design from the Academy of Art University where she also embarked on an MFA in fashion design. Dr. Avery's fashion studies began in Los Angeles at Compton College where she facilitated art & dance. Her culminating project earned first place while enrolled at LA Trade Tech for fashion illustration.

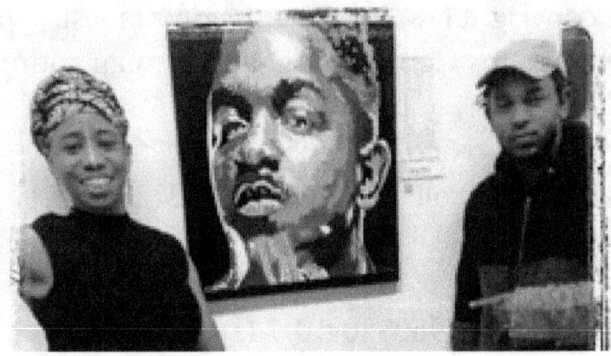

Photo credit: Cleveland Palmer Long Beach, CA

Sharoné Seaberry earned her associate degree in psychology from Georgia Military College. She then went on to obtain her bachelor's degree in psychology & human services at Clayton State University in Georgia. While at CSU, Sharoné also studied art history, drawing, and digital art design. Her love for art and helping others go hand-in-hand.

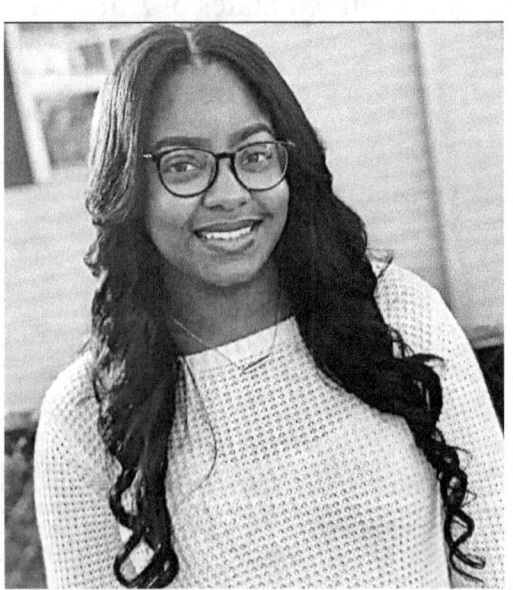

Photo credit: Maliyah Martin Red Jacket, West Virginia circa 2017

AGE LEVEL:

THIS BOOK IS DESIGNED FOR ELEMENTARY LEVEL STUDENTS/CHILDREN.
ALTHOUGH, TEENS, MOMS & OTHER ADULTS ARE WELCOME TO CREATE!

Directions!

Are you ready to be creative? Here are simple directions to make paper doll magnificence! Be sure to ask a trusted adult to assist you with the process. (Any word in bold print is a vocabulary word with the definition in parenthesis. There are also picture descriptions of each emboldened word towards the end of this booklet).

1.   Gather materials: You will need "safe" scissors, a pencil, clear tape, a white eraser, and coloring utensils (crayons/colored pencils/ water-color-pencils/water-based markers/water-based paint/ "safe" paint brushes, and a small cup of water.) Be sure your workspace is completely shielded with a protective covering.

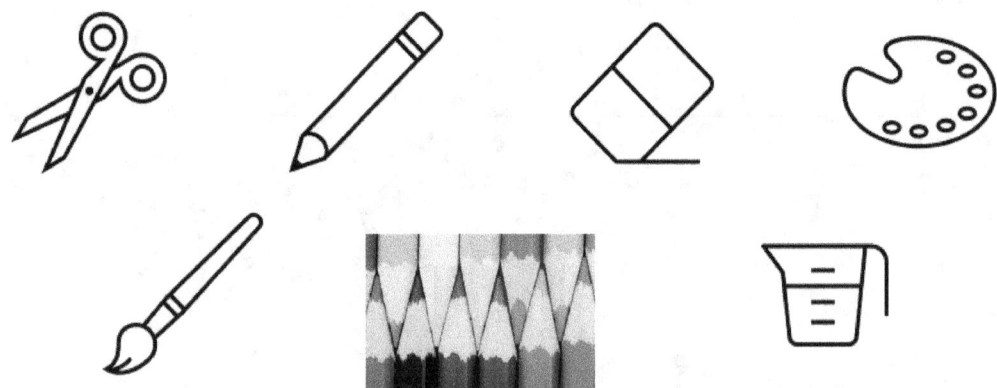

2.   Cut-it-out: Carefully, cut out the fashion **croquis** (an expressive drawing of the human body that fashion illustrators place unique fashion designs on) to the left. This will be your paper doll. Each doll has a name. Cut along the **contour** (solid outside line in black). Then, cut out the outfits. WARNING: DO NOT cut off the tabs attached to the drawings. You will need them to dress the croquis.

3.   Color: Decide what colors you would like to utilize (use) or make. Then, add those colors. If you'd like to mix paint colors, a chart is on the last page. You can practice directly on that page, before applying the colors out on your paper **garbs** (clothing).

Warning!

1.   Keep band-aids close, in case of a paper cut. Ouch! Those hurt!

2.   Be sure young children are aided by a trusted adult when working with materials!
Be safe, and have fun!

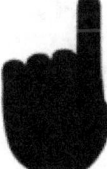

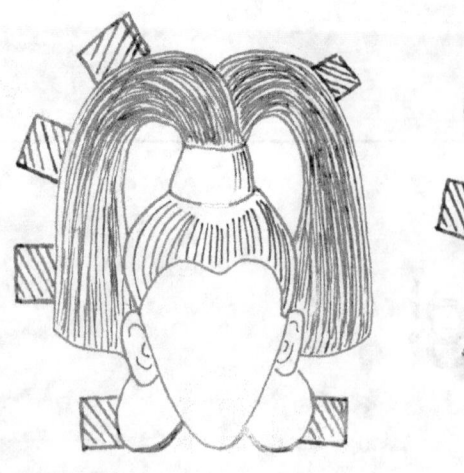

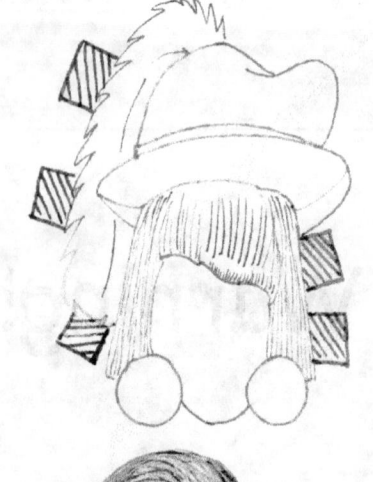

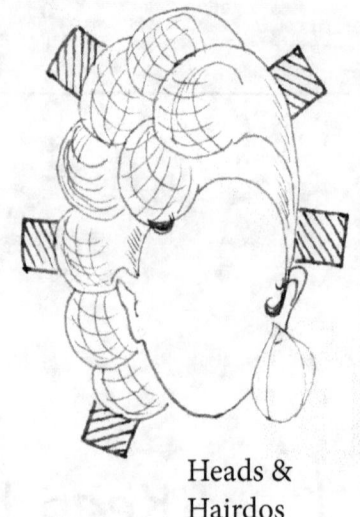

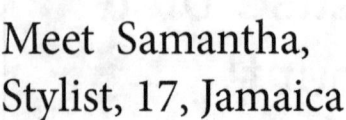

Heads &
Hairdos

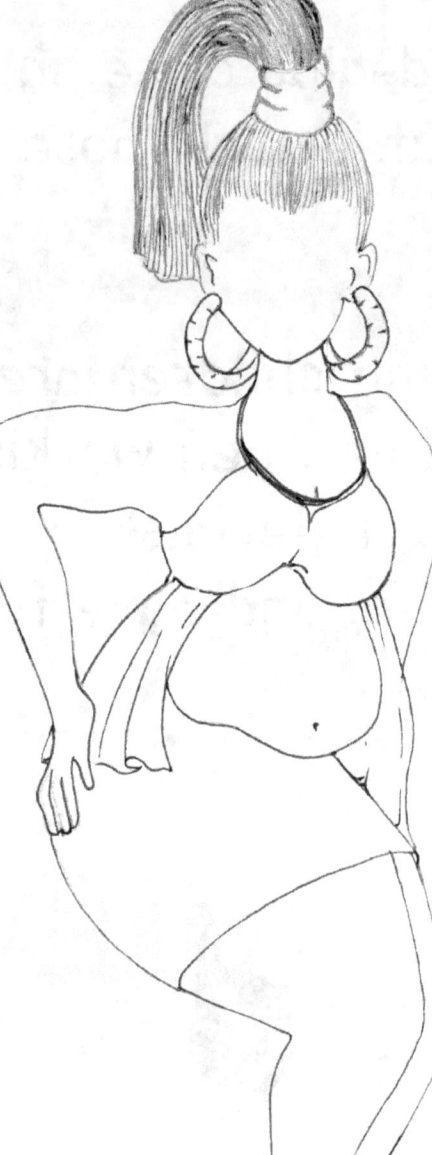

Meet Samantha,
Stylist, 17, Jamaica

Hi, my name is
Samantha from
Jamaica. When I'm
not on the beach,
like today, I enjoy
traveling to places
like New York City
and styling busi-
nesswomen with
designs from my
online shop.

I'm a freshman at
Lorgan State
University.

When you create
my **hue**, maybe
you can make me
look like you?

Have fun!

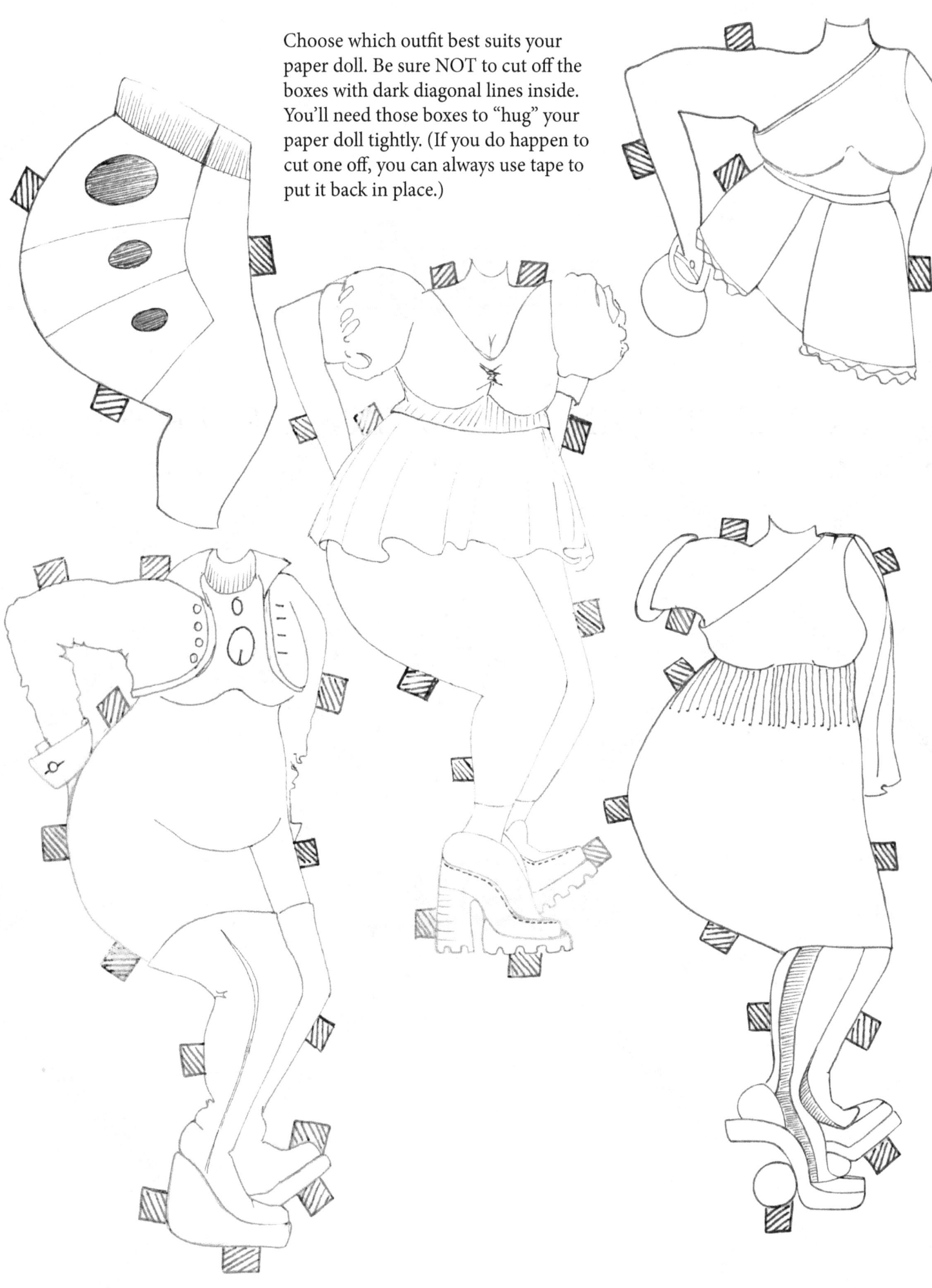

Choose which outfit best suits your paper doll. Be sure NOT to cut off the boxes with dark diagonal lines inside. You'll need those boxes to "hug" your paper doll tightly. (If you do happen to cut one off, you can always use tape to put it back in place.)

PAGE LEFT BLANK FOR CUTTING PURPOSES

PAGE LEFT BLANK FOR CUTTING PURPOSES

Hey, my sunshines!
My name is Joy, and I'm a fitness instructor at
my own gym: Divine Ladies Fitness. When I'm
not instructing, I love to strut the runway.

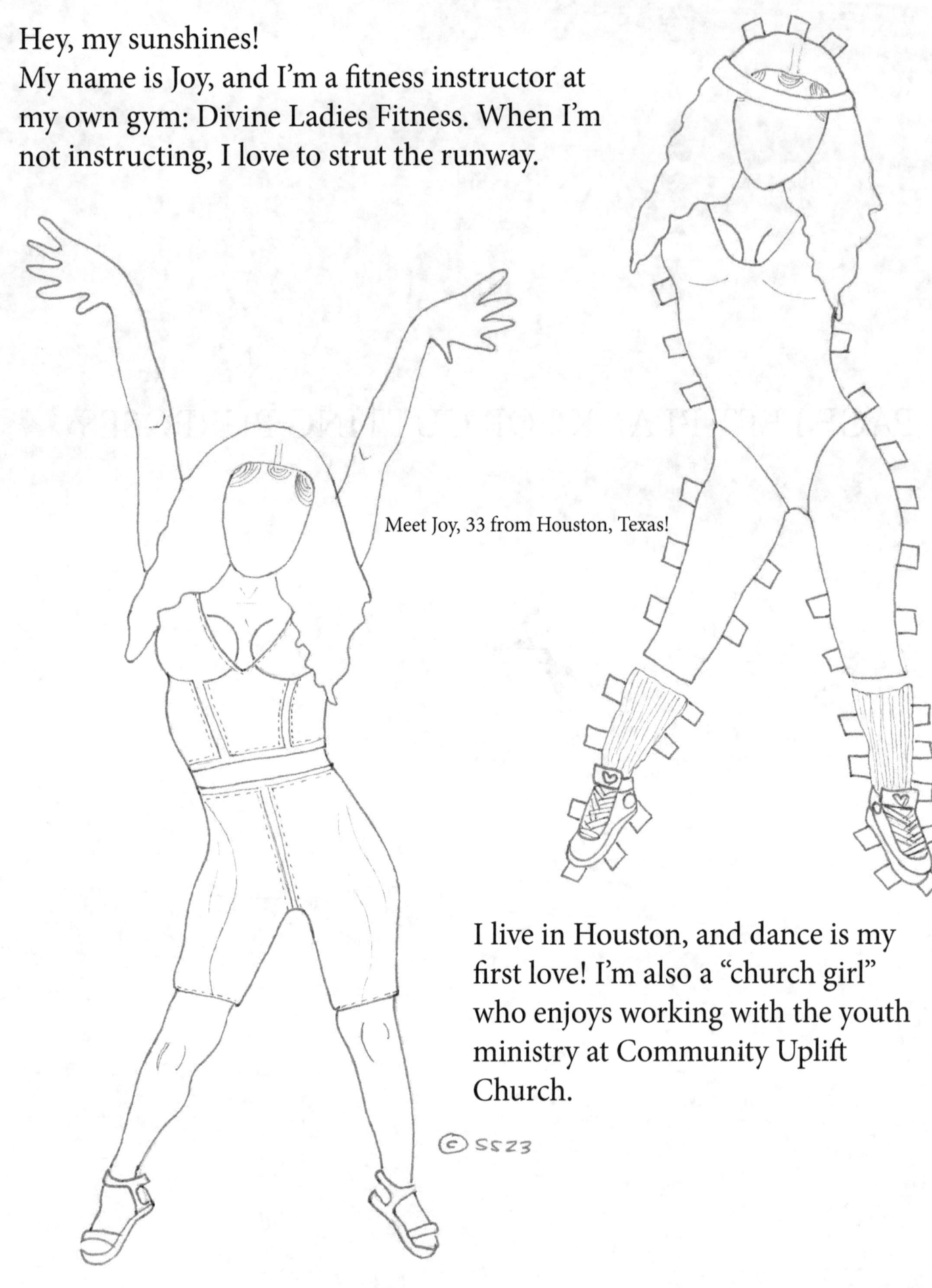

Meet Joy, 33 from Houston, Texas!

I live in Houston, and dance is my
first love! I'm also a "church girl"
who enjoys working with the youth
ministry at Community Uplift
Church.

© SS23

Be sure to cut out all of the flaps. You will need them to "hug" your croquis!

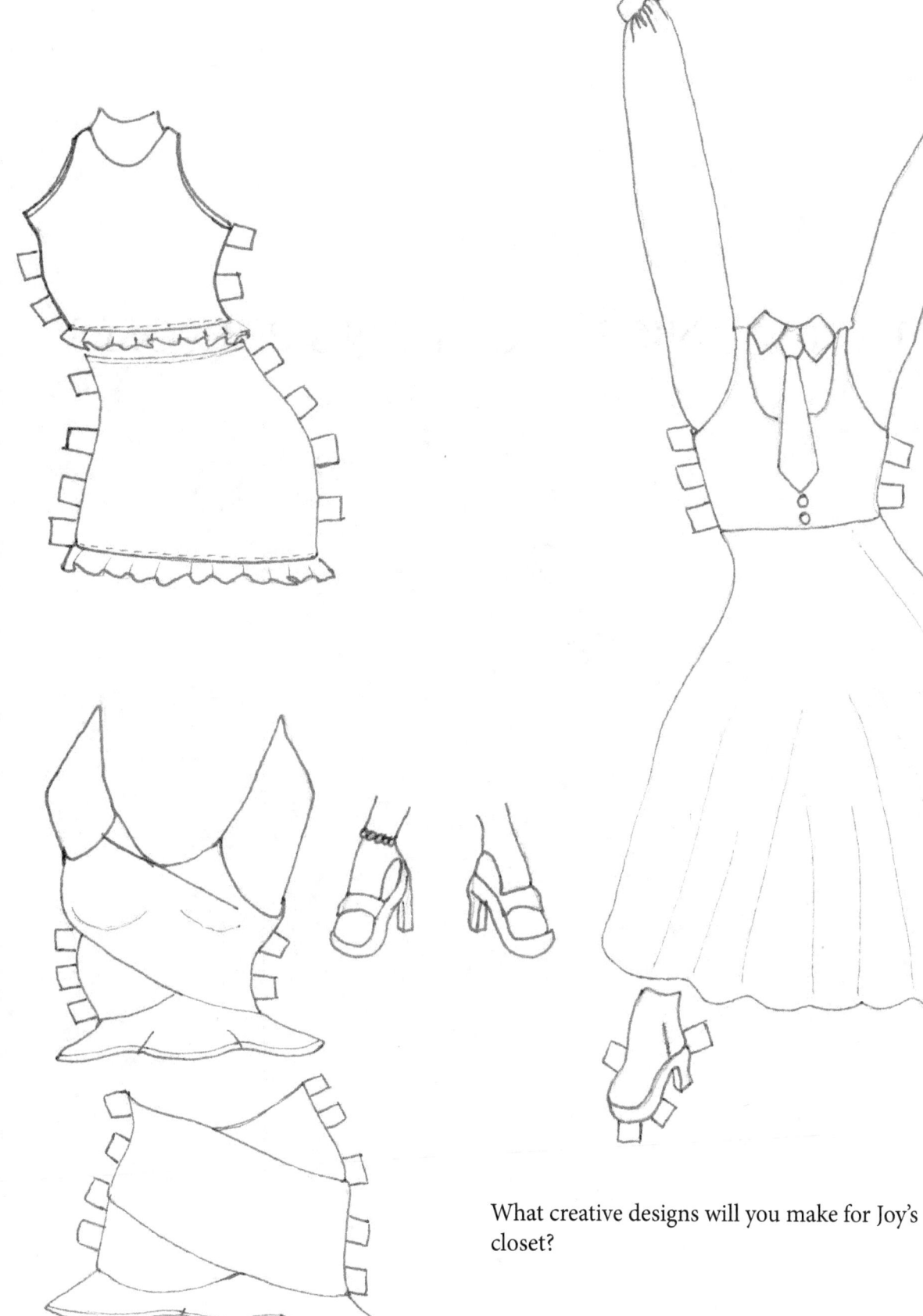

What creative designs will you make for Joy's fashion closet?

PAGE LEFT BLANK FOR CUTTING PURPOSES

PAGE LEFT BLANK FOR CUTTING PURPOSES

Heads & hairdos!

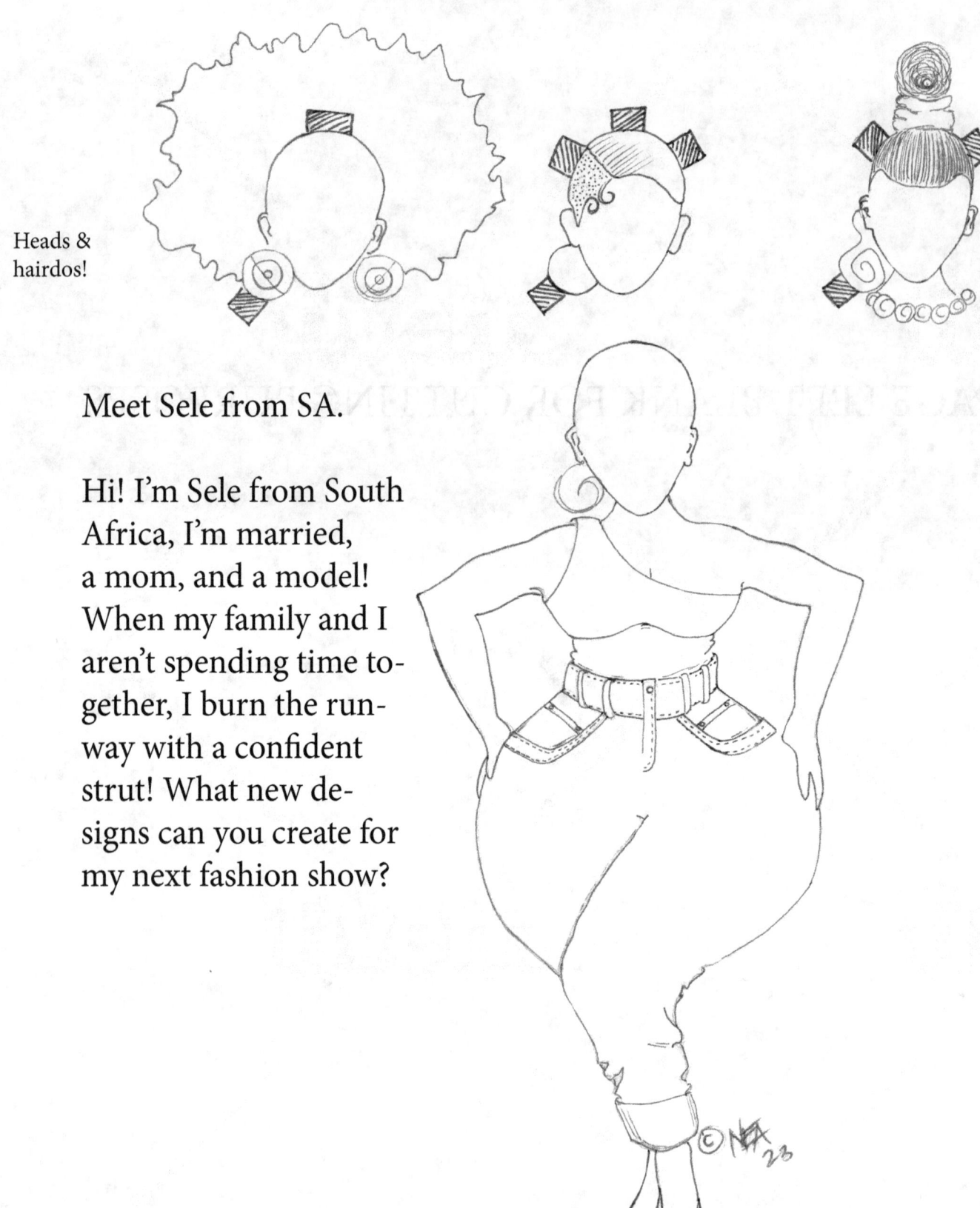

Meet Sele from SA.

Hi! I'm Sele from South Africa, I'm married, a mom, and a model! When my family and I aren't spending time together, I burn the runway with a confident strut! What new designs can you create for my next fashion show?

Which outfit will you choose, first? Be sure to cut the entire piece out along with the boxes!

There are even accessories for you to choose from! (Shoes and purses)

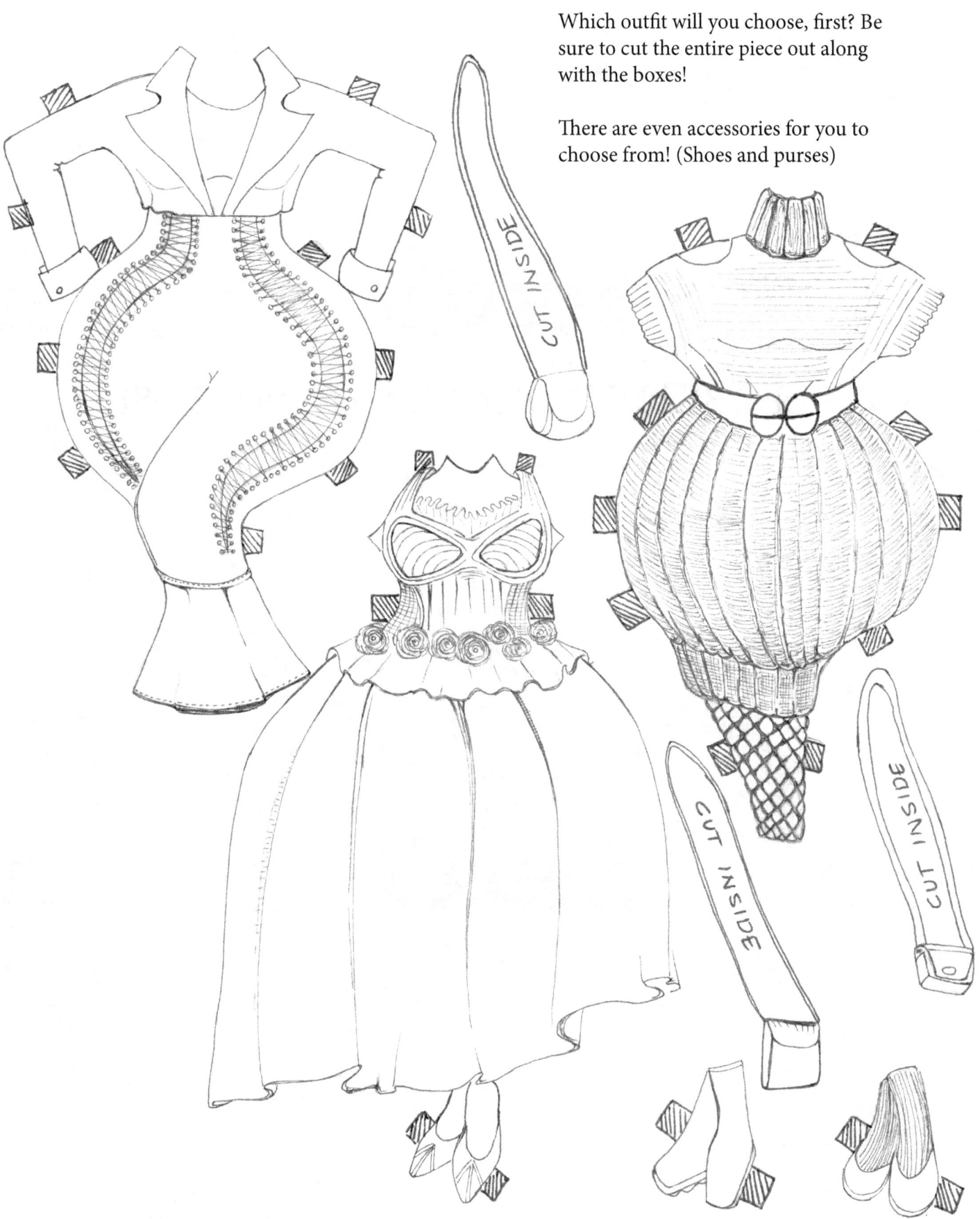

What shoes will you choose when combining them with an outfit?

PAGE LEFT BLANK FOR CUTTING PURPOSES

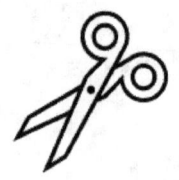

PAGE LEFT BLANK FOR CUTTING PURPOSES

Meet Shayna, 23, from
Atlanta, Georgia!

Hey, come shake it up
with Shayna! I'm a beau-
ty/fashion influencer
and an amazing artist!

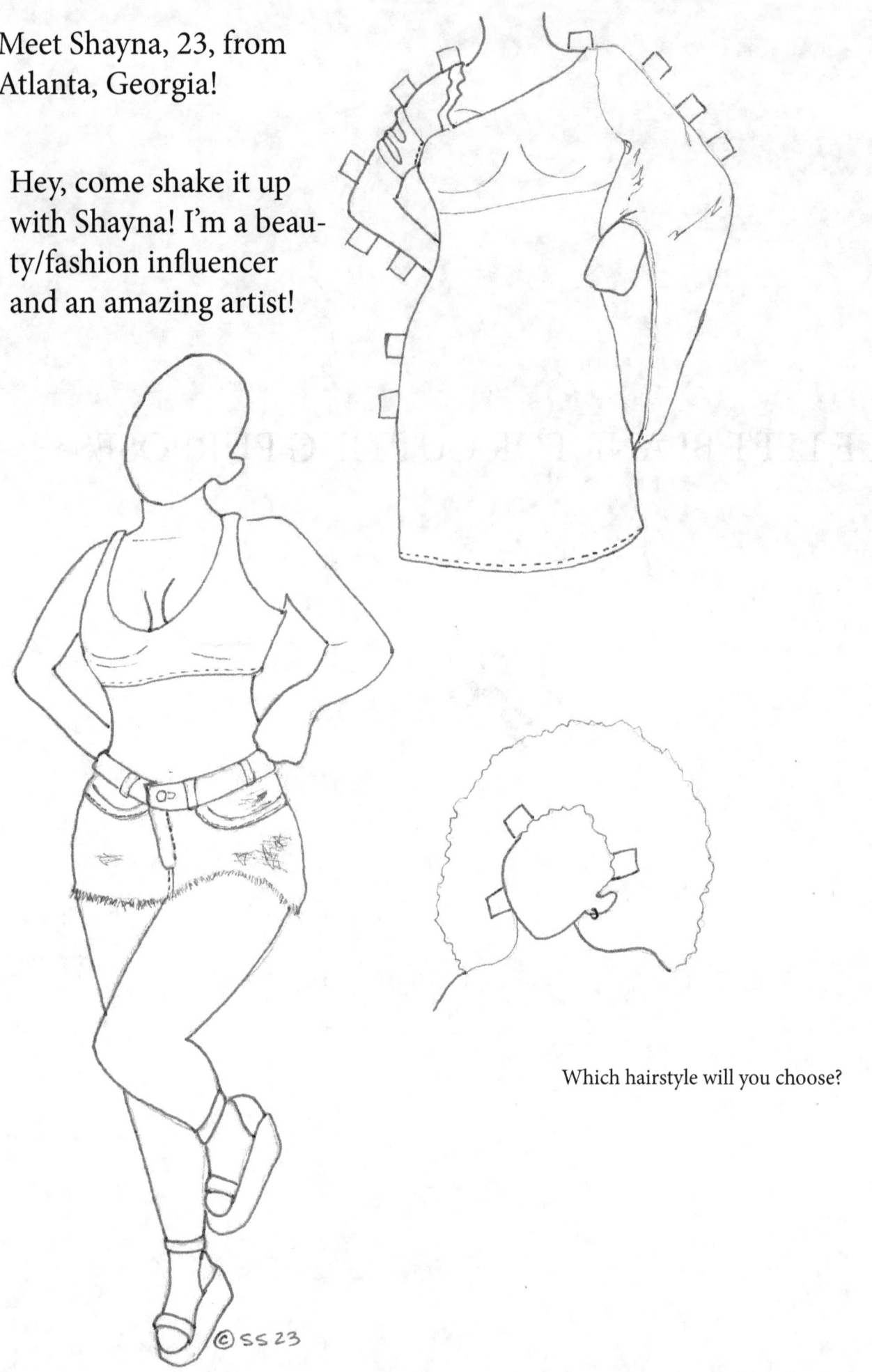

Which hairstyle will you choose?

© SS 23

Which hairstyle will you choose?

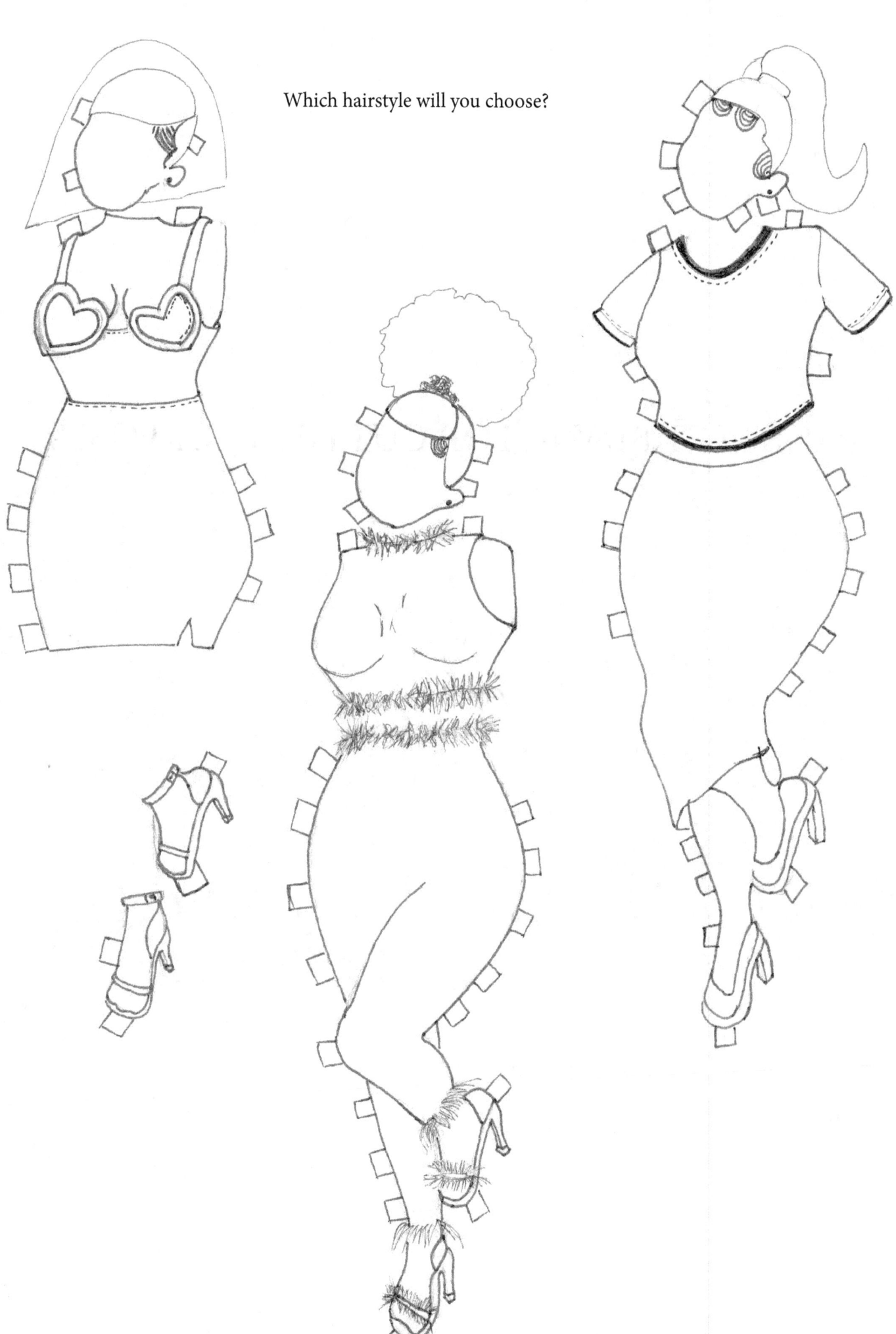

PAGE LEFT BLANK FOR CUTTING PURPOSES

PAGE LEFT BLANK FOR CUTTING PURPOSES

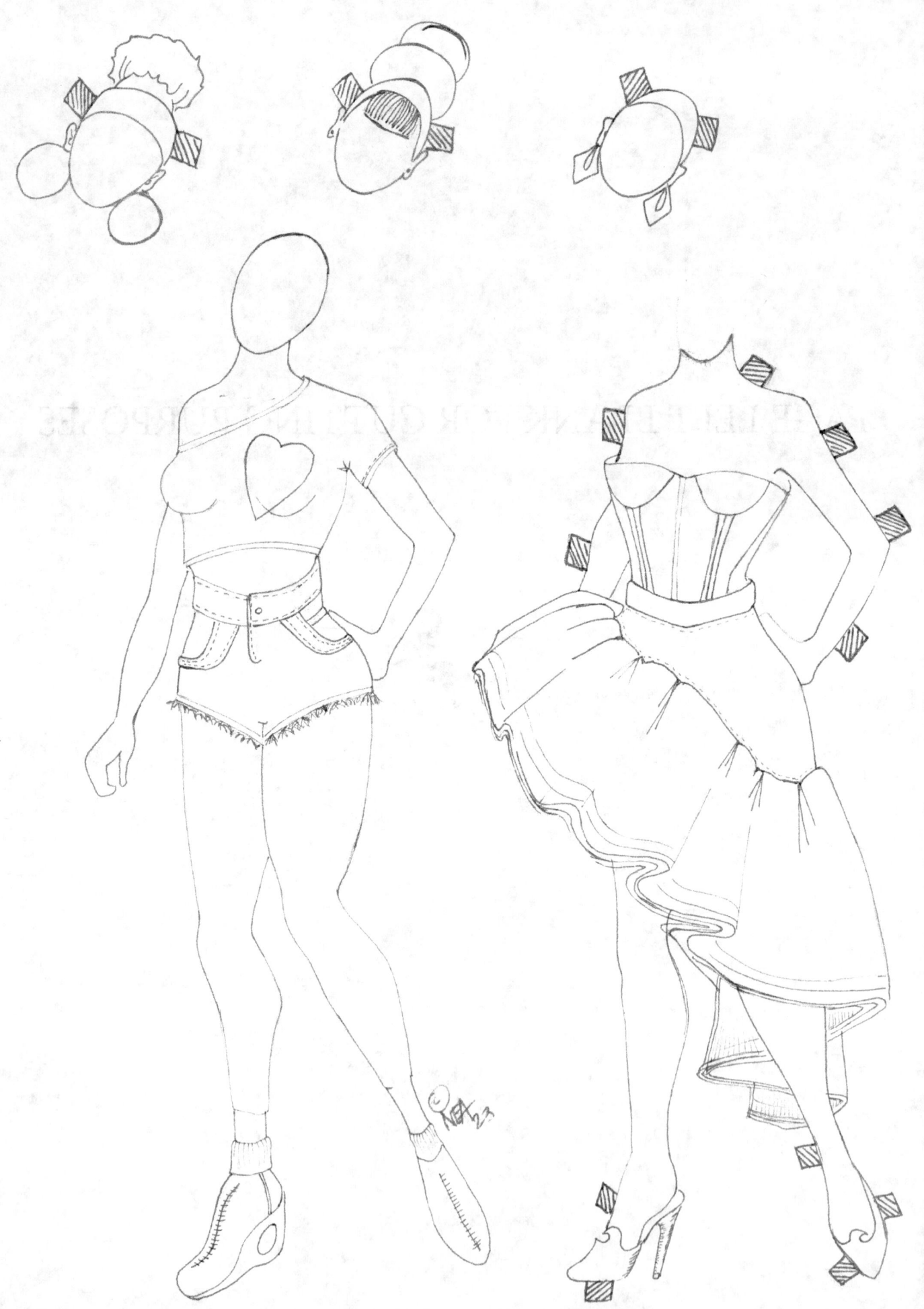

Meet AJ, MUA, LA, 23

I'm AJ. As a professional make-up artist, I'm able to work on movie sets around the world. When I'm not on set, I'm walking the red carpet, attending industry events, and costume parties.

How will you make my wardrobe come alive? What type of faces will you create? Will you add onto the present hairstyles?

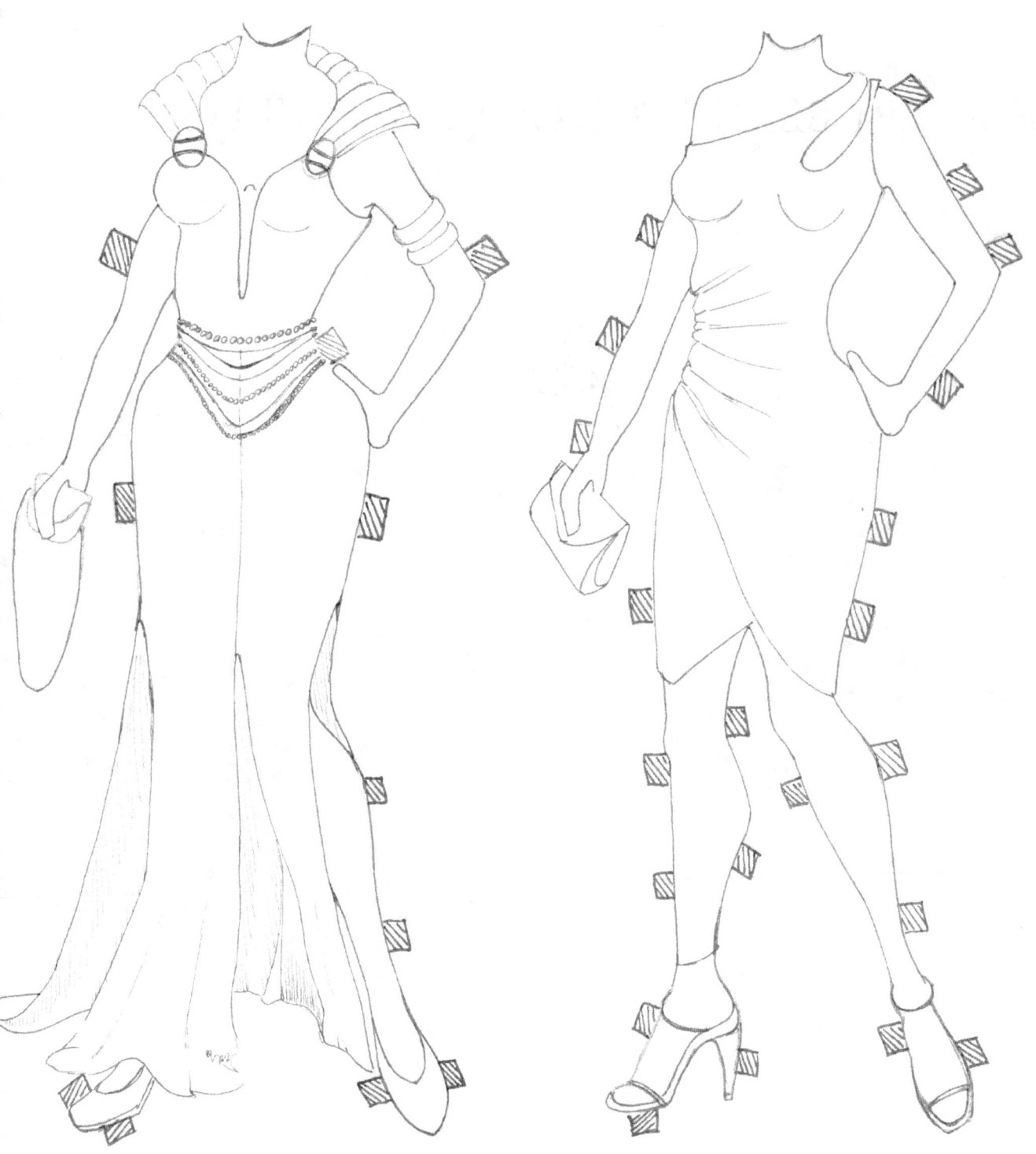

PAGE LEFT BLANK FOR CUTTING PURPOSES

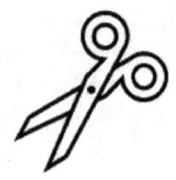

PAGE LEFT BLANK FOR CUTTING PURPOSES

Hi, my name is Sydney! I'm a 10th grader attending Star Gems Performing Arts Academy (a high school in North Philly) with a passion for fashion! I aspire (hope) to become a fashion designer once I graduate college.

Meet 15 yr. old Sydney from Pennsylvania!

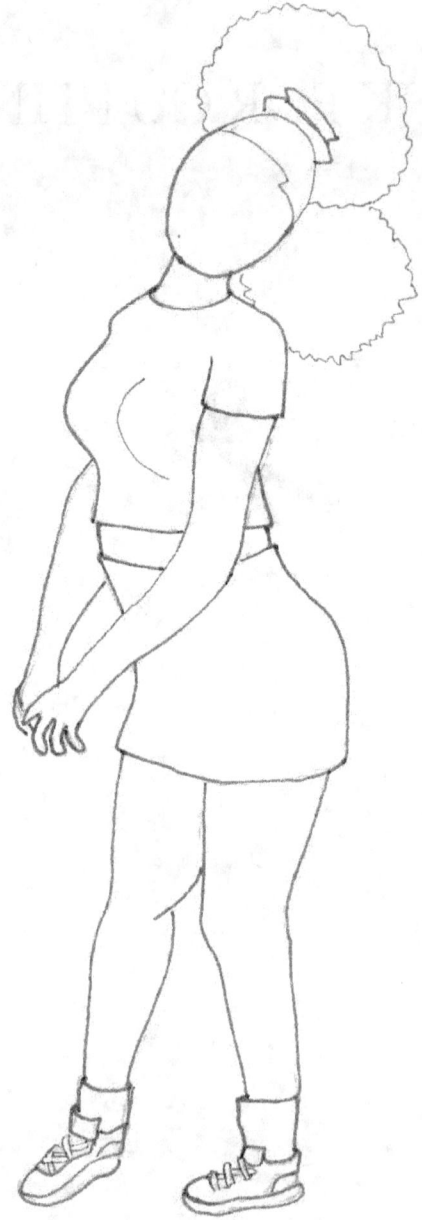

What kind of ideas do you have for Sydney's new wardrobe? What colors will you use? Any new hairstyles you'd like to try?

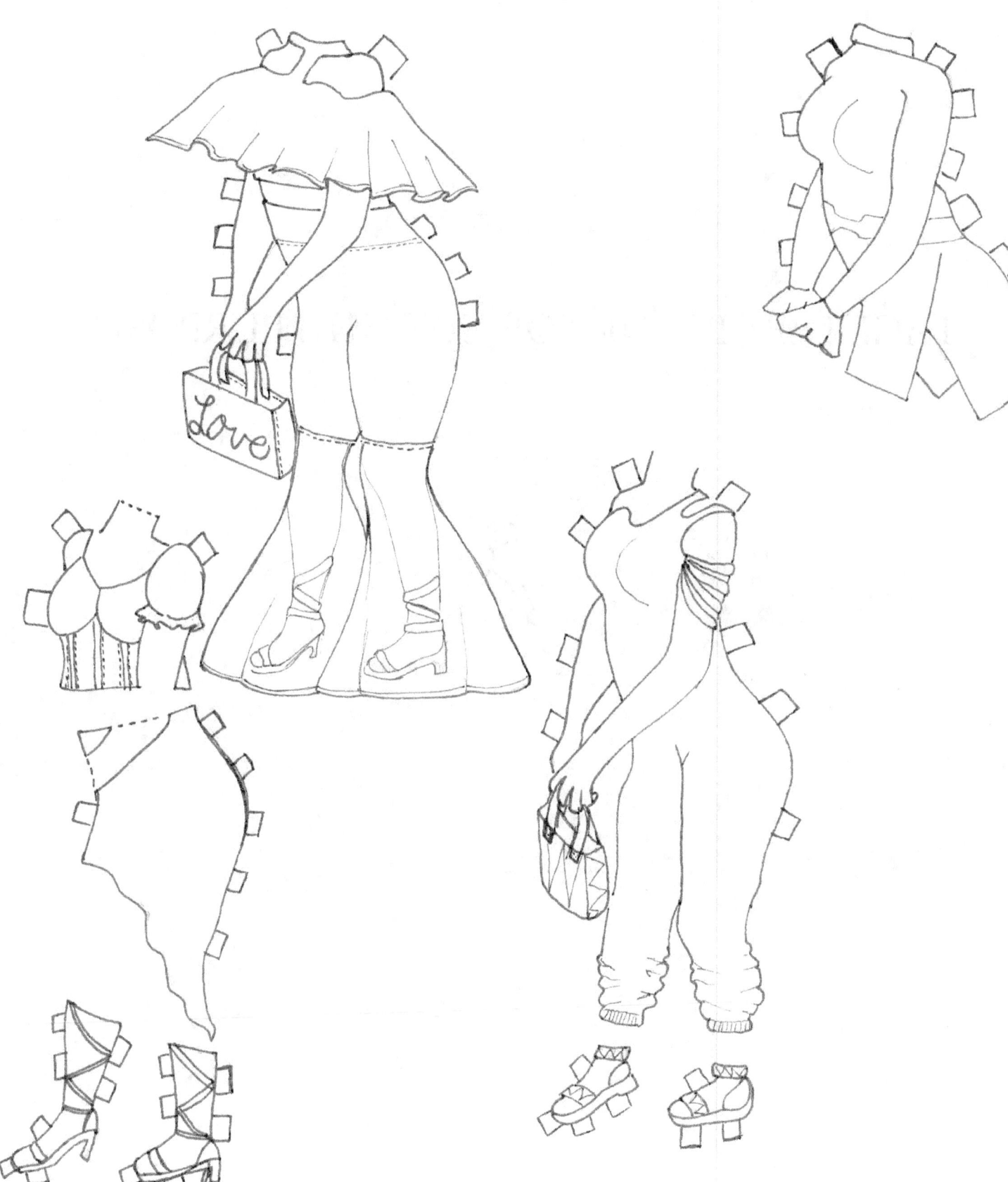

PAGE LEFT BLANK FOR CUTTING PURPOSES

PAGE LEFT BLANK FOR CUTTING PURPOSES

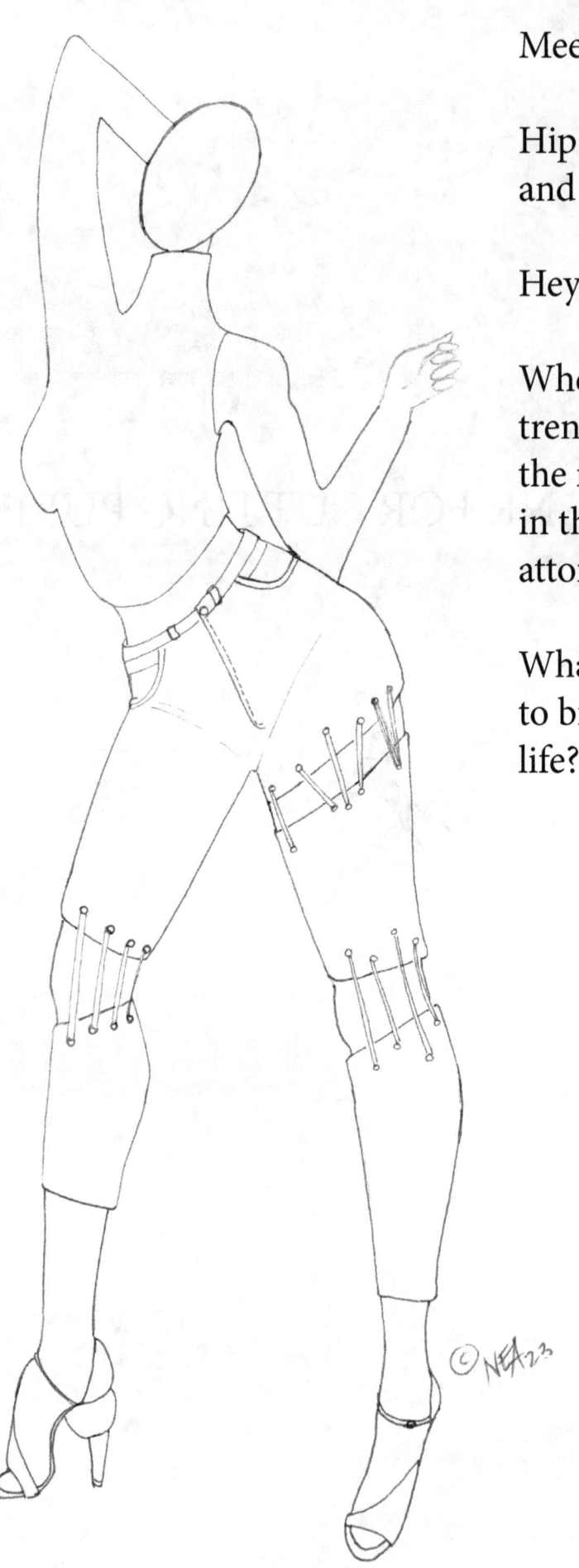

Meet Nikki from NYC

Hip Hop dancer, model, and lawyer, 27

Hey, there! I'm Nikki.

When I'm not dancing to trendy beats, I'm owning the runway, or delivering in the court room as an attorney-at-law.

What colors will you use to bring each outfit to life?

©NEA23

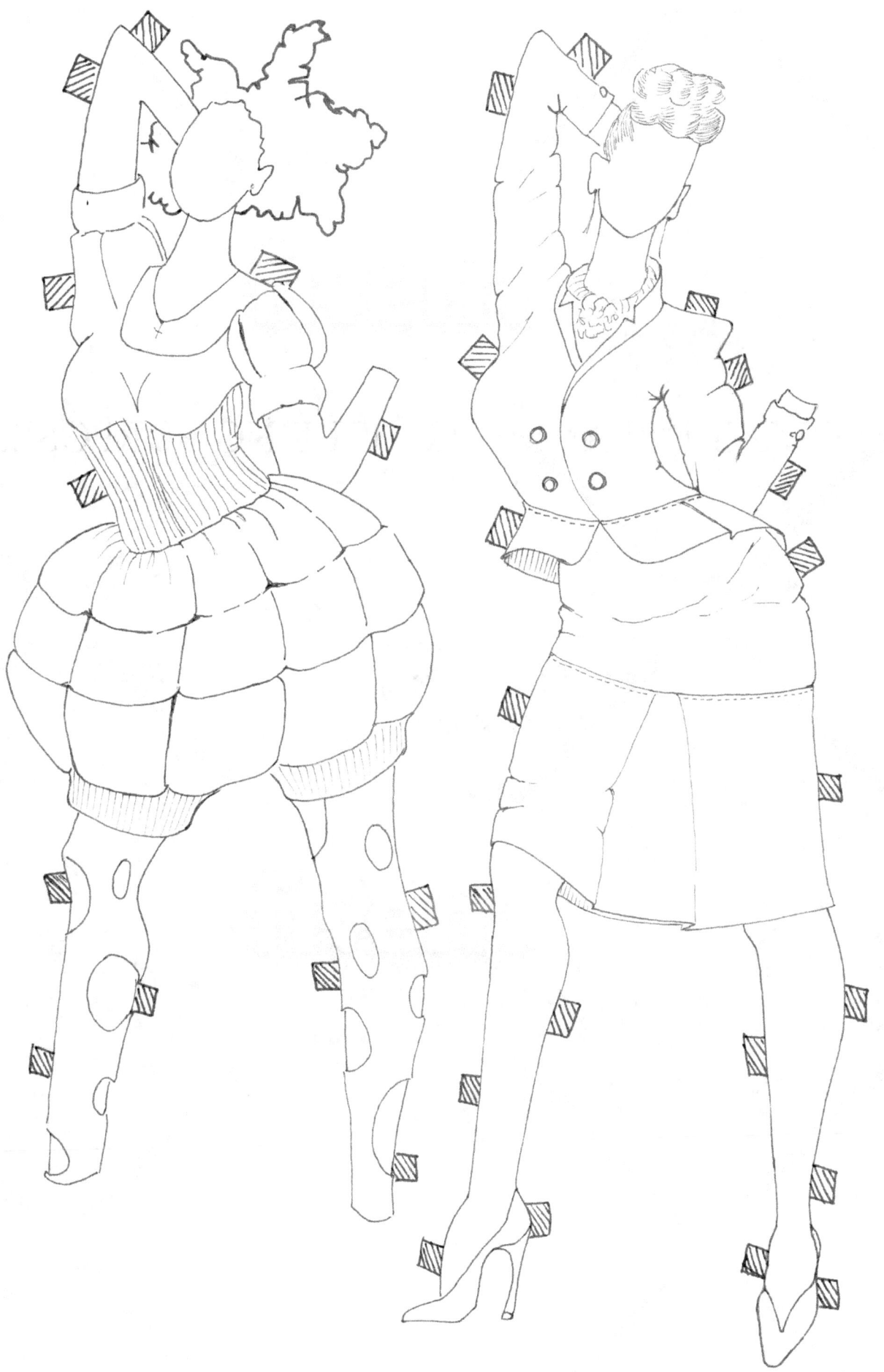

PAGE LEFT BLANK FOR CUTTING PURPOSES

3c's

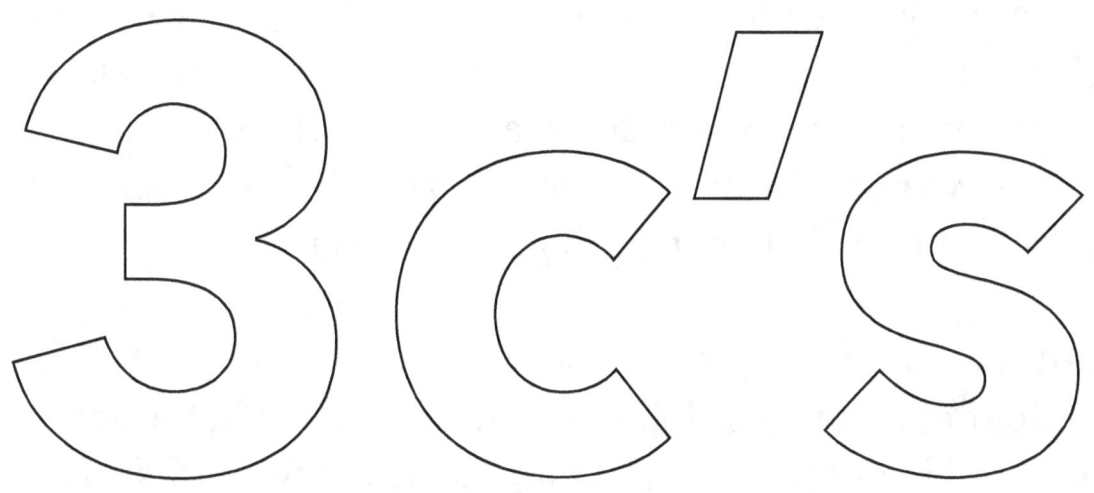

Color.

Cut.

Create!

Design your own wardrobe!

We hope you are enjoying our Black Girl Glory™: We Sparkle paper doll cut-outs! Now, it's time for YOU to create your very own designs. If you've ever wanted to be a fashion designer, here is where it begins with pen & paper! We've provided the next seven pages for you to show-off your creativity. Below are a few steps to get things started!

1.   Trace-it! Based on the name of the croquis at the top of the page, trace the contour of that paper doll from the neck down in the appropriate box. You should have room to trace at least two new outfits and/or accessories and heads (face + hairdo). Don't forget to add tabs!

2.   Find inspiration! You can utilize fashion magazines, social media screenshots, old sketches you have, or ideas from your head!

3.   Using your inspiration, draw your fashion ideas directly onto the new croquis you drew. Anything you don't like, you can erase and re-do! Be sure not to simply copy. Add a few things or take away a few. You want your designs to be as original as possible!

4.   Color, color, color! You've had practice; now it's time for you to shine. Add color. Refer to the color chart on the last page for a quick reminder.

5.   Cut-it-out! Using safe scissors carefully cut out your design(s).

6.   Warning! Without flaps on the **perimeter** of your design, you cannot dress your paper doll. (In case you forgot to add tabs, draw tiny squares, separately. Then cut them out. Next, sit the tab on the sticky side of the clear tape. Place the taped tabs around the edge of your fashion designs. Voila! You **mended** your paper clothing.

TRACE YOUR **"Samantha"** PAPER DOLL IN THE SPACES PROVIDED TO
MAKE NEW OUTFITS. USE THE SMALLER RECTANGLES FOR
ACCESSORIES.

PAGE LEFT BLANK FOR CUTTING PURPOSES

TRACE YOUR **"Joy"** PAPER DOLL IN THE SPACE PROVIDED TO MAKE NEW OUTFITS. YOU CAN USE A SMALL PORTION FOR ACCESSORIES.

PAGE LEFT BLANK FOR CUTTING PURPOSES

TRACE YOUR **"Sele"** PAPER DOLL IN THE SPACES PROVIDED TO MAKE
NEW OUTFITS. USE THE SMALLER RECTANGLES FOR ACCESSORIES.

PAGE LEFT BLANK FOR CUTTING PURPOSES

TRACE YOUR **"Shayna"** PAPER DOLL IN THE SPACE PROVIDED TO MAKE
NEW OUTFITS. YOU CAN USE A SMALL PORTION FOR
ACCESSORIES.

PAGE LEFT BLANK FOR CUTTING PURPOSES

TRACE YOUR **"AJ"** PAPER DOLL IN THE SPACES PROVIDED TO MAKE
NEW OUTFITS. USE THE SMALLER RECTANGLES FOR ACCESSORIES.

PAGE LEFT BLANK FOR CUTTING PURPOSES

TRACE YOUR **"Sydney"** PAPER DOLL IN THE SPACE PROVIDED TO MAKE
NEW OUTFITS. YOU CAN USE A SMALL PORTION FOR
ACCESSORIES.

PAGE LEFT BLANK FOR CUTTING PURPOSES

TRACE YOUR **"Nikki"** PAPER DOLL IN THE RECTANGLE PROVIDED TO MAKE A NEW OUTFIT. USE THE SMALLER RECTANGLES FOR ACCESSO-RIES.

WAYS TO BE SUSTAINABLE...

1. In an effort to be sustainable, you can make additional outfits out of old newspaper or the backs of printing paper you are no longer using. Always remember, never be wasteful.

2. You can also laminate your paper doll and paperdoll clothes to keep them for years to come. You may even pass them down to your little siblings or your own children one day!

3. Try pasting your croquis onto cardboard to keep them in good shape.

4. Be sure to recycle any unwanted paper clippings or disgarded paper items.

Picture-Dictionary

Below is a list of words used throughout the book. The images denote/express the meaning of the word. Can you add any words to the list and draw your own definition?

1.   accessories- pocketbook, shoes, hand bag, earrings, hat etc,

2.   contour- Outer line; the imaginary line that runs along the edge of an object, body or facial features.

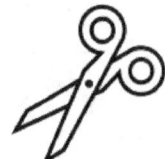

2.   garb- Special clothing; religious and other; outfit

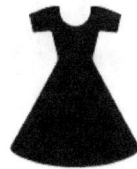

3.   mend- repair; repair a piece of clothing

4.   perimeter- the space directly outside of an object or place's contour. Travel alongside. The letter "x" below is on the perimter of the square.

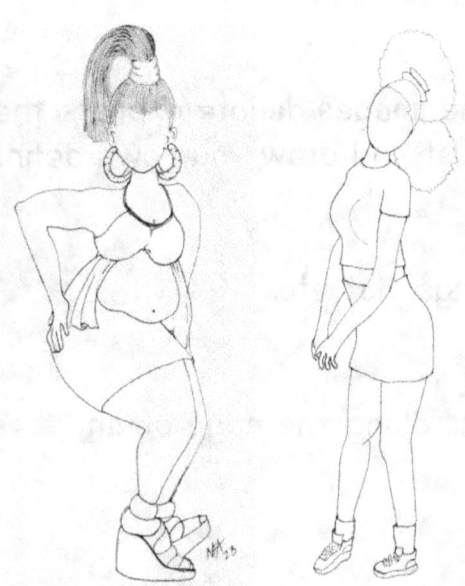
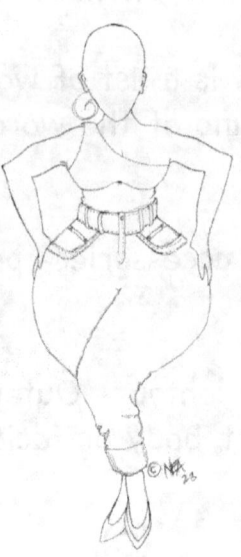

**THANK
YOU FOR
YOUR
PURCHASE!**

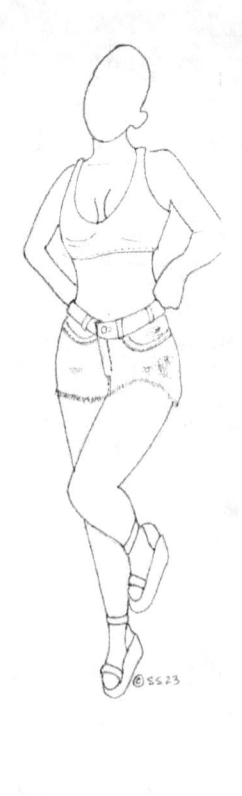
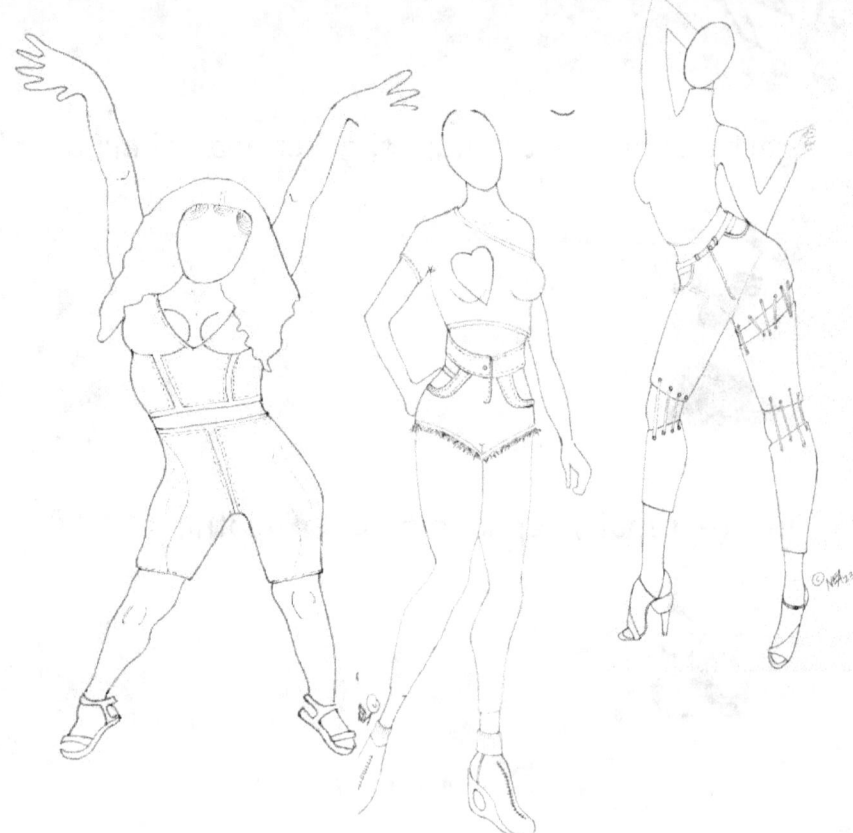

BLACK GIRL GLORY™

COLOR MIXING

Whether you are using acrylic paint, water color paints/pencils, colored pencils, try mixing the colors below to make new colors!

Blue + Yellow = Green

(The more blue you add, the darker green you'll get)
(The more yellow you add, the lighter your green)

Yellow + Red = Orange

(The more yellow you add, the lighterer the orange)
(The more red you add, the darker your orange)

Red + Blue = Purple

(The more blue you add, the darker green you'll get)
(The more yellow you add, the lighter your green)

Adding a tiny bit of white to a color can make it a lighter shade. Adding brown or a tiny bit of black can make a color a shade darker.